THE APE CRUSADERS

SEAN WHYTE

HALSGROVE

British Library Cataloguing-
in-Publication Data
A CIP record for this title is
available from the British Library

ISBN 978 0 85704 124 1

HALSGROVE

Halsgrove House,
Ryelands Business Park,
Bagley Road, Wellington,
Somerset TA21 9PZ
Tel: 01823 653777
Fax: 01823 216796
email: sales@halsgrove.com

An imprint of Halsgrove Ltd.
Registered in England No. 6029724
Information on all Halsgrove titles is
available at: www.halsgrove.com

Printed in Italy by Grafiche Flaminia

FSC
www.fsc.org
MIX
Wood from
responsible sources
FSC® C007907

INTRODUCTION

THROUGH NO FAULT OF ITS OWN one of our closest living relatives is careering towards extinction.

As a species it elicits a deep admiration and respect among many, so much so it is among the top ten most popular wild animals in the world. Why, then, is this auburn-haired relative of ours being persecuted mercilessly into extinction? There are a number of factors responsible but the primary one has to be loss of habitat.

In the past twenty or so years the main cause of deforestation has been a rapid and massive expansion of oil palm plantations, some legal, many not. Fly east to west in Kalimantan (the Indonesian part of Borneo – the third largest island in the world) a distance of nearly 1000kms and you will see more oil palm plantations than forest. This ruthless development of the palm oil industry has been made easy by an Indonesian government which shows nothing but contempt for the natural environment. But then, it has to be said, the palm oil industry which includes multi-national household names did nothing to rein in their destruction of both forests and wildlife until public awareness of thousands of orangutans being killed every year brought pressure to bear.

At the forefront of showing consumers the price paid by orangutans as well as many other species like tigers and elephants for the palm oil used in their biscuits, cereals and numerous other household products, have been the Centre for Orangutan Protection (COP) and Nature Alert.

COP was formed by Hardi Baktiantoro and close friends in 2007. With nothing more than experience and a fiery passion for saving orangutans, they committed to do all they could to save a species which their own government seems set on wiping out. Genocide is an emotive word, but this appears to be the unwritten policy of the Indonesian government; 125,000 legally protected orangutans killed or captured and sold into the illegal wildlife trade over the last forty years without a single prosecution, says it all.

If the Indonesian government wanted to enforce the law, saving orangutans would be a lot easier.

The work of COP is often dangerous, always arduous and never welcomed by the government of Indonesia. The Ape Crusaders stay away from home and their families for long periods, often relying on strangers in remote locations offering them food and a roof over their heads for the night. Their pay is very modest but their passion for saving orangutans is huge. COP's main area of operation is Kalimantan, all 539,460 sq.km. Often, though, they are called to help rescue illegally held orangutans or those in zoos on the island of Java.

The purpose of this book is not to try and educate anyone about the biology or distribution of orangutans, all of which are copiously covered in a myriad of other books and on the internet. The objective is to illustrate the problems and show what it takes to even begin to try and resolve them. It's about the work of a very dedicated group of people doing their best against all the odds to save a very special animal from persecution and extinction.

The Ape Crusaders are often the orangutans' only hope. No one but COP travels the length and breadth of Kalimantan and Java exposing illegal logging, naming and shaming greedy palm oil companies, investigating the illegal wildlife trade and helping orangutans kept in horrific zoos. What they see and have to attend to in one day would be enough in one lifetime for most people. I know, because I have travelled extensively with the Ape Crusaders and, like them, I have had many sleepless nights, experienced some massive emotional lows as well as some close calls with danger.

The reality of what it takes to save orangutans is what I hope to have portrayed. I doubt very much you have seen anything like this in a book before. If this makes you sad or angry, please use these emotions to spur yourself on to do more to help save this most remarkable great ape by helping COP: www.orangutanprotection.com and www.orangutan-appeal.org.uk

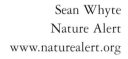

Sean Whyte
Nature Alert
www.naturealert.org

ACKNOWLEDGEMENTS

THE AUTHOR WISHES TO THANK the Centre for Orangutan Protection Ape Crusaders who unselfishly give so much of themselves to saving orangutans. It has been my great privilege to travel extensively throughout Kalimantan with many of them, witnessing for myself scenes such as those illustrated in this book which I know they often face day after day; I have seen and felt the emotional strain this places on them. I know I speak for a great many others when I say how much I admire what they do.

I would like to thank my wife Margaret for her support and patience with my orangutan obsession over the past twenty years and for her help with the production of this book.

Photos are taken by the Centre for Orangutan Protection and the author.

Orangutan Appeal UK is a registered charity based in the UK dedicated to the preservation of orangutans and protection of their habitat. The Appeal strives to protect remaining populations of orangutans by providing support and funding for projects across Malaysian and Indonesian Borneo and by raising awareness of this great ape across the globe.

The charity is totally independent of Nature Alert and all other conservation organisations, but where possible it does support projects which help save orangutans and their habitat. Trustees and supporters of Orangutan Appeal UK are proud that it was the first sponsor of the Centre for Orangutan Protection (COP) back in 2007 when it provided them with the Ape Crusader rapid response vehicle, which amongst other things has to date enabled some 50 orangutans to be rescued. The Appeal has supported COP projects in each subsequent year, and in 2011 a second rapid response vehicle, the Ape Defender, was provided by Orangutan Appeal UK supporters enabling COP's rescue and investigative work to increase throughout Indonesian Borneo.

MAP OF MALAYSIA & INDONESIA

VIETNAM

CAMBODIA

PHILIPPINES

SOUTH CHINA SEA

Sulu Sea

MALAYSIA

Kota Kinablu • • Sandakan

BRUNEI   SABAH

MALAYSIA

• Kuala Lumpar

SARAWAK

• Tarakan   Celebes Sea

Sibu •   EAST
KALIMANTAN

Kuching •

SINGAPORE •

Singkawang •

Pontianak •   WEST
KALIMANTAN   BORNEO

• Bontang

• Samarinda

SUMATRA

CENTRAL
KALIMANTAN   • Balikpapan

Ketapang •

Palangkaraya •

SULAWESI

• Amuntai
SOUTH
KALIMANTAN

Banjarmasin •

Bandu Sea

INDONESIA

Java Sea

• JAKARTA

INDIAN OCEAN

JAVA   • Semarang

N
W   E
S

THE ORANGUTAN

DESPITE BEING LEGALLY PROTECTED throughout its range in Malaysia and Indonesia, despite being one of our closest relatives, despite being one of the most popular animals on the planet, despite being Asia's only great ape, the orangutan is being ruthlessly exterminated.

Living only on the Southeast Asian islands of Borneo and Sumatra, orangutans are divided into two distinct species: the Sumatran orangutan and the Bornean orangutan. In the Malaysian state of Sabah (northern Borneo) there are thought to be 10,000 remaining, down from about 40,000 in the late 1960s while next door but also part of Malaysia, Sarawak has some 2-3000 orangutans left, mostly in national parks. Although disappearing at an alarming rate, Kalimantan (the Indonesian part of Borneo) has about 42,000 remaining and Sumatra 6600. With the annual killing rate of 3000-5000 over the last forty years, the orangutan's future looks extremely bleak.

The finger of blame for the demise of the orangutan can be pointed firmly at the respective governments. It is they who sell the forests, home to orangutans as well as countless other species. It is the very same governments who show no interest in enforcing the law which on paper gives this species total protection.

In the meantime the Centre for Orangutan Protection (COP) does what it can against all the odds, but as you are about to see from this book, they are active, successful and passionate about their work; big organisations could learn a lot from them. You won't find another organisation like COP.

WEST KALIMANTAN

Left: About to be loaded onto an aircraft in Western Kalimantan (Indonesian Borneo) and taken to a rescue centre in Central Kalimantan – at that time the nearest refuge for rescued orangutans.

Orangutan Appeal UK were COP's first sponsor.

Opposite: Having arrived in Central Kalimantan these orphaned baby orangutans are inspected before being taken to the nearby rescue centre.

Palm nuts from the oil palm tree.

Palm oil production is arguably the most environmentally destructive industry on the planet, causing massive devastation to rainforests and wiping out wildlife and indigenous communities all over Malaysia and Indonesia.

No one is seeking a ban on palm oil. It is, after all, a very versatile oil used all over the world in a myriad of different products. The chances are many of the household products you buy contain palm oil. Many brands of biscuits, breakfast foods, chocolate, bread, soap and a whole lot more all contain palm oil – often labelled as palm extract or vegetable oil.

If you do not want to consume food or use soap etc tainted with the blood of thousands of dead orangutans and a great many other wild animals, demand from your supermarket they label palm oil clearly in their ingredients.

11

Sintang, North West Kalimantan. COP and Nature Alert visited this remote region in February 2010 where we discovered many illegally held captive orangutans. These two were chained up hungry and thirsty outside a restaurant. We always travel with fruit and water to hand out.

A tip-off in February 2010 led COP and Nature Alert to this private home.

To the right of the garage we found this three to four year old female. The owner said he bought her from a logging company.

Even the Bupati (Head of the District) of Sintang had an illegal pet orangutan outside his residence.

Solitary and chained to the cage floor with nothing but bare wires to sleep on this four year old orangutan appeared to be in a state of shock.

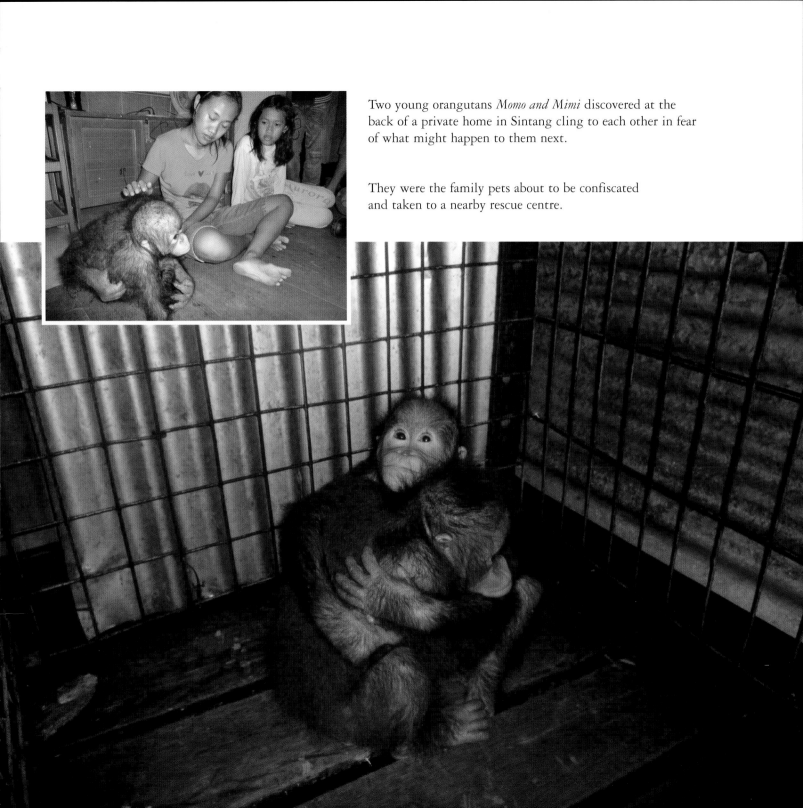

Two young orangutans *Momo and Mimi* discovered at the back of a private home in Sintang cling to each other in fear of what might happen to them next.

They were the family pets about to be confiscated and taken to a nearby rescue centre.

Opposite: Momo and Mimi (l-r) looking a lot happier and healthier now they are in a rescue centre.

As of 2011 there are at least 1200 orangutans in rescue centers throughout Indonesia, with many more, mostly orphaned babies, waiting for a space to become available. It has been estimated that for each orangutan in a rescue centre at least another five will have been either killed, died during capture or while being held as a pet.

Right: The cherished pet of this boy, baby *Kerrie* as she came to be known was under-nourished when found by COP and Nature Alert. The next day she was confiscated by the local forestry police.

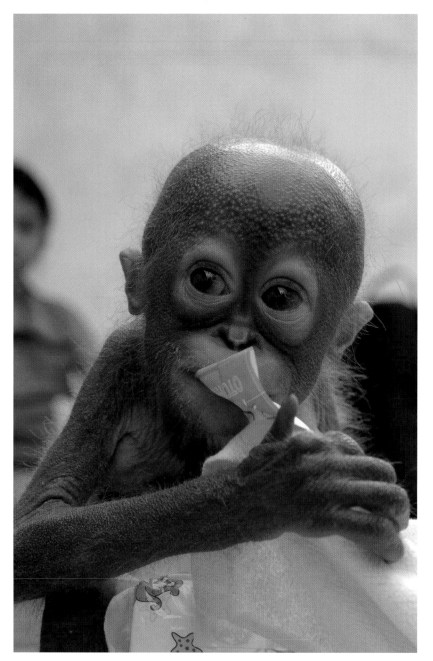

The many adorable faces of *Kerrie* disguise the trauma she experienced of being in her mother's arms when she was killed with either a machete or a gun.

Kerrie quickly stole the hearts of everyone she came into contact with, including the head of the local forestry police in Ketapang.

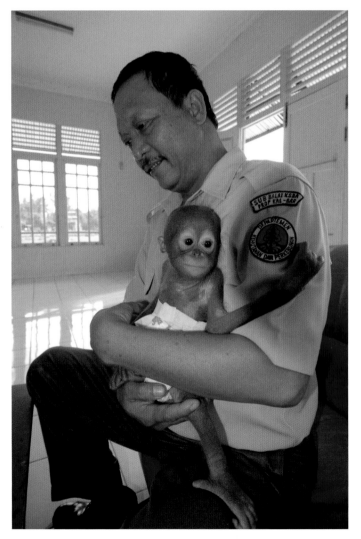

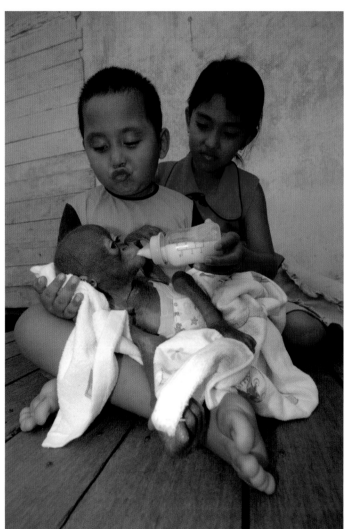

Grandchildren of the caretaker at the local rescue centre happily took turns to feed *Kerrie*.

The nearest orangutan rescue centre involved a forty minute flight followed by a six hour road trip, all of which *Kerrie* handled well. A few months later we learnt *Kerrie* had died from breathing complications while at the rescue centre.

Barges laden with wood constantly ply the coastal waters off Ketapang, South West Kalimantan, a region notorious for both legal and illegal logging, mostly to make way for new oil palm plantations.

80% of all logging in Indonesia is illegal.

Following up a television report, in March 2010 COP and Nature Alert went to find *Mely*, a gentle female orangutan who had been chained up for almost all her life at a riverside home in Sambas, North West Kalimantan.

Mely relished the company of Hardi. It was as if she knew he had come to help her.

Following a newspaper appeal *Mely* was rescued soon after by International Animal Rescue and taken by river, road and air to their centre.

A shelter was eventually erected over this female orangutan – *Lupis* – though the cage was far too small and situated alongside a rubbish dump.

Opposite: Lupis, thought to be about 17 years of age, was one of two large orangutans held in small cages but out of sight of one another (see over page) on a small housing estate in Pontianak, West Kalimantan. Realizing the cages were too small the owner offered to give up the orangutans to any rescue centre who would take them. The size of these adult orangutans meant they would require much larger cages, better still an outside enclosure, but no rescue centre was able to accept these two and in late 2011 they were sent to a zoo whose orangutan cages were even worse.

This beautiful, friendly
male orangutan named
Lupus was found on the
same estate as *Lupis* (see
pages 26 and 27) surviving
in this tiny cage devoid
of all enrichment, unable
to escape the burning sun
in the afternoon, and with
no water to drink.

After we had fed *Lupus* lots
of fresh fruit he was ready to
sleep clutching in one hand
cherries we had given him but
he was now too full to eat.

Pongo had been chained like this for a long time before being found and rescued by COP. Washing an orangutan may look strange but they often are forced to sleep in their own stale food and faeces. Washing removes the risk of infection transmission and most rescued orangutans do enjoy it!

Neng was at death's door when rescued near Sintang by COP and Orangutan Outreach.

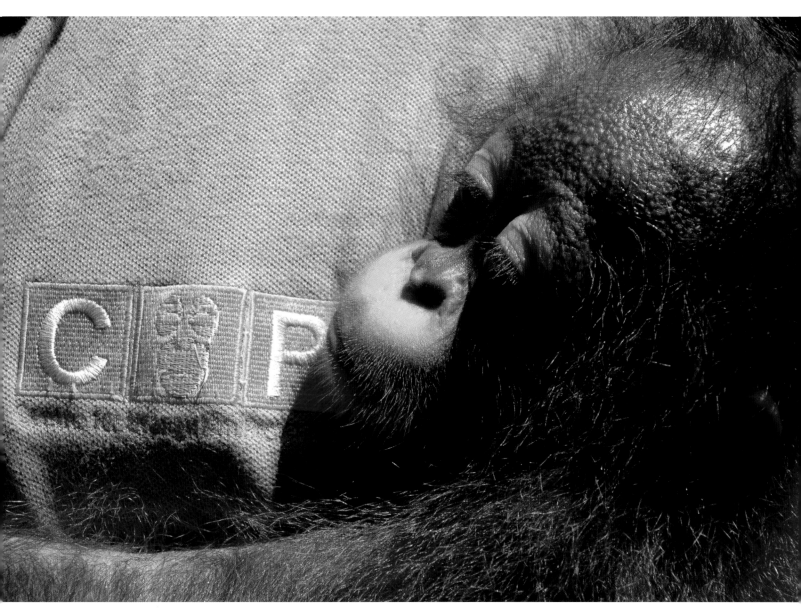

Only one organisation travels the length and breadth of Kalimantan (Indonesian Borneo) and Java rescuing orangutans: The Centre for Orangutan Protection. They are only able to do so because of the support they receive from Orangutan Appeal UK and others.

In return for some fruit and attention Hardi was rewarded with a display of affection. One of a number of orangutans rescued by the local authorities and given to this tourist resort in West Kalimantan.

Opposite: Newly rescued this baby enjoys its first fresh fruit in a long time.

The Indonesian government admits deforestation has led to the death of 3000 orangutans per year since the 1970s.

Chained and confined in the most appalling conditions *Jojo's* rescue by COP came not a minute too soon.

Opposite: On route to rescue an orangutan the Ape Crusaders are often severely tested by road conditions as here in West Kalimantan.

This three year old male orangutan named *Bembi* had been kept as a pet in a village near Ketapang, West Kalimantan. He was confiscated (see opposite) and taken to a nearby rescue centre.

Right: Children watch as the two orangutans are taken away by the Ape Crusader rescue team.

Below: A Ketapang forestry police officer confiscating two baby orangutans. Confiscations are often made a long way from base and any back-up help which might be needed, so where possible it is always advisable to use friendly persuasion rather than force.

Ketapang, South West Kalimantan. Following a tip-off about an illegal orangutan at the back of a home used also as a hairdressing salon, Hardi occupied the hairdresser by having his hair cut while I went out the back to see what I could find.

At the back of the house I found *Habibie*. She had spent five years chained up like this. Two days later she was confiscated by the forestry police.

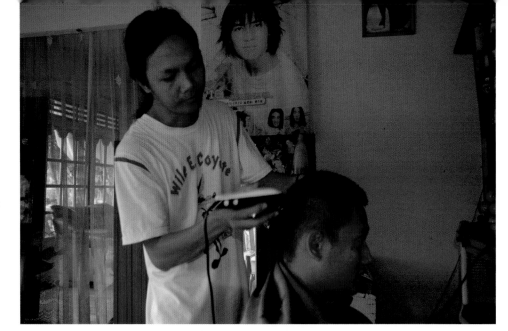

Hardi holds the fruits of the oil palm tree which are the cause of such widespread devastation across Borneo and Sumatra and now spreading to other countries with an equatorial climate.

These small, subsistence farmers can be found over much of Kalimantan and Sumatra. No one wants to deprive them of earning a living from growing oil palm trees. It is the national and multi-national companies who are the main cause of deforestation.

RESCUING ORANGUTANS TAKES BOTH PHYSICAL AND EMOTIONAL STRENGTH

To assess their level of fitness and ability to work as a team new recruits to COP undergo a challenging trek.

Left: No one said it would be easy.

Below: Teamwork.

Above: The team has bonded.

Right: Relief it's the end of the day.

CENTRAL KALIMANTAN

There is never any lack of interest when COP talk to local villagers about orangutans. Although some landowners succumb to 'get rich quick' offers from oil palm companies who want their land, most would prefer to preserve their forests which provide them with a free source of food, shelter and clean water.

More often than not travel by boat is the only option. These lifejackets were donated by an Australian supporter.

Armed only with cameras COP are on the way to document illegal logging. Never without risk and almost always a long way from help.

Opposite: Engaging with and receiving interest from local communities, particularly children, is vital for the long term future of orangutans.

Often the best way to travel through remote areas is by motorcycle and this one was provided by the Australian Orangutan Project. Flooded roads are common and makeshift rafts provide local entrepreneurs with an opportunity to make some much needed money.

Once safely on the raft this COP investigator can enjoy the ride!

Palm oil kills as Christopel Stone, often called Pak Elok, knows better than most. Pak Elok has maintained his ancestral forest for sixty-five years. At seventy-eight years old he visits Jakarta to support the COP public awareness campaign.

A scene repeated all over Borneo, day in day out. Forests cleared to make way for a new oil palm plantations.

Indonesia Corruption Watch has estimated the Indonesian economy lost Rp 71 trillion ($8.16 billion) from 2005-09, or $1.6 billion annually, due to deforestation. Human Rights Watch puts the losses even higher, at $2 billion a year.

49

Opposite: Hardi Baktiantoro documenting illegal logging in Central Kalimantan. The evidence gathered was used in a campaign that saved some 50 orangutans and 5000 hectares of forest.

Australia legally imports around A$840million worth of illegal timber products each year, much of it from Indonesia, which means people buying furniture or building materials in Australia are likely to be directly contributing to the logging of rainforests and the deaths of millions of animals – including orangutans, tigers, and elephants.

Right: The forest destroyed, young oil palm plants now replace the ancient trees and all wildlife.

A show of unity from local villagers in Central Kalimantan hoping to save what remains of their forest to the right of the photo.

Opposite: Opet, a baby happy to have been rescued by COP near Pangkalan Bun, Central Kalimantan.

Making way for new oil palm plantations. The ownership of palm oil companies is worldwide, but Malaysian companies are very prevalent in Indonesia while at the same time trying to look good in the media by claiming not to be causing deforestation in their own country.

Left: Ape Crusaders trying to keep a palm oil company from destroying more forest and orangutans.

COP found two orangutans were being kept in this wooden cage at a village in Central Kalimantan, with no room to move, no water, little food and no protection from either the blazing heat or torrential rain.

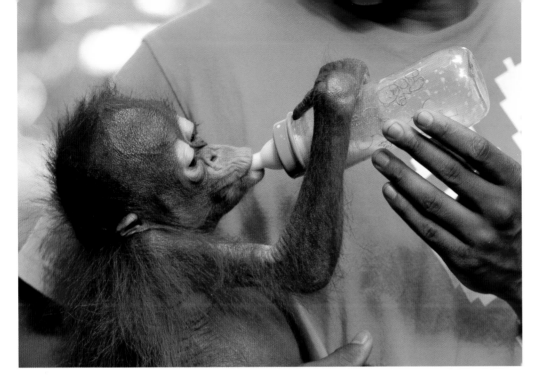

Baby *Ottoh* was found suffering from malnutrition in Pamalihan village, Central Kalimantan.

Ottoh had been kept as a pet for six months so it was important for COP to explain to the village children why she was being confiscated and taken to a rescue centre. A total of three baby orangutans were discovered in this one village.

A police officer from the Agency for Nature Resource Conservation (BKSDA) of Central Kalimantan holds *Ottoh* prior to her transfer to the Orangutan Foundation International Care Centre for Orangutans.

Following up a report of an orangutan being held illegally deep inside a forest, COP's Rapid Reaction Team rescue staff face all kinds of hazards – waterlogged trails being a common one.

When the rescue team arrives they are often confronted with sights like this – a baby orangutan is incarcerated between these logs.

"I saw a pair of innocent eyes staring at me while eating leaves between pieces of chopped wood, which were stacked in a way to resemble a cage. I squatted down and looked at her eyes for a couple minutes. She looked skinny with dots of her own dried faeces stuck on the tip of her orange shaggy hair. "
From the COP rescuers' field report.

Patai village, Central Kalimantan.

Even poor people living in remote areas often know killing or capturing an orangutan is illegal.

Epa is given her first drink of milk since her mother was killed and the only affection shown to this very young baby comes from her COP rescuer.

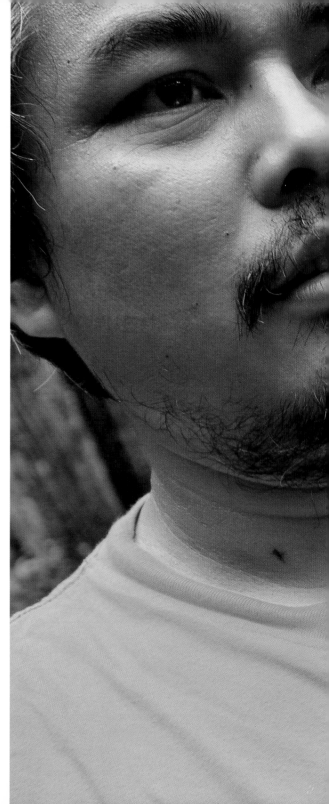

Can you even begin to imagine how many trees once stood here? How many birds, animals and insects once roamed freely through the forest?

Producing palm oil is arguably the most environmentally destructive industry on this planet. I can think of no other which has destroyed so many animals, so much plant life and often illegally. Almost singlehandedly in Indonesia the palm oil industry is driving orangutans, tigers, rhinos and elephants towards extinction. Sean Whyte, Nature Alert

The Ape Crusader is an invaluable asset to COP. Frequently used in rescues and visiting locations with illegal loggers.

"But thus far, the government appears to have little stomach for taking on illegal forest activities. The Forestry Ministry, together with law enforcement agencies, has processed just 58 of the 8,000 cases of illegal mining and plantation operations reported in 2010."
The *Jakarta Globe*, 28 March 2011

Checking for pot holes and water depth before the Ape Crusader vehicle proceeds.

COP investigators enter the stunningly beautiful Katingan forest in Central Kalimantan. Palm oil companies want to tear down this forest.

Local villagers show their support for COP. 'Stop Sawit' translates to Stop Palm Oil, meaning in this instance stop palm oil companies from taking more of our land.

The protest moves to outside the home of the Governor of Central Kalimantan in Palangkaraya.

The Ape Crusader Rapid Response Team
in action across all terrains.

Logs are normally sent downriver to be processed or exported, but some are sawn on site for local use.

View from Sentuai Hill, Central Kalimantan, showing recently logged forest in the distance.

Forestry Minister Zulkifli Hasan says the government will recycle old permits and allow the conversion of up to 3 million hectares of forests into plantations – despite a recent moratorium. Jakarta Post 29 April, 2011

A school visit to the Tura village in Central Kalimantan. Winning the hearts and minds of children is often the key to protecting the environment and the orangutans. The best way to do this is through education and example.

Po'o, a nine year old male orangutan suffering from malnutrition. His mother was shot by a poacher. COP rescued *Po'o* and took him to a nearby rescue centre.

Despite having full legal protection at least 125,000 orangutans have been illegally killed or captured and sold into the illegal wildlife trade since the 1970s. No one has ever been prosecuted.

Left: A new palm oil plantation camp in Kuala Kuayan, Central Kalimantan – where *Po'o* and his mother once roamed freely over pristine rainforest.

Below: Baby *Opet's* physical condition was surprisingly good, suggesting she had been very recently orphaned.

Forest fire destroying what was once primary rainforest inhabited by orangutans in Central Kalimantan.

Opposite: Illegally logged timber like this is used to make furniture, especially garden furniture, all over the world. The USA, New Zealand and Australia are big importers of stolen wood.

Making way for another oil palm plantation. Scenes like this are very common throughout much of Kalimantan. In many locations it is almost impossible to see rainforest in any direction. All wildlife either killed, captured or driven away.

The British "Unreported World" award winning documentary television crew filming with COP in Central Kalimantan in March 2011.

Opposite: A palm oil nursery. The company has for a long time also been trying to log the surrounding forest which is home to amongst other things, about 200 orangutans. COP are helping local people resist approaches from the palm oil company.

EASTERN KALIMANTAN

When kept as a pet, orangutans often have to sleep in their own faeces, urine, stale food etc, so whenever possible it is advisable to wash them as infections are always a risk to the Ape Crusaders and orangutans already in the rescue centre where they are taken.

Opposite: Freshly washed two-year-old *Alex* clings to Hardi and has a nap. Found by COP in Wanasari Village, Muara Wahau, East Kalimantan, he and his mother are, like almost all in this book, victims of the palm oil industry.

Whenever possible, to protect both orangutan and rescuer from any cross infection, it is safer to wear gloves and a facemask when rescuing orangutans.

People who keep orangutans as pets rarely give them anything to drink, which is why the Ape Crusaders go prepared.

Look at those eyes. Imagine what she has already gone through in her short life and try to imagine what she is thinking.

A rainforest teeming with wildlife once stood here but has long since been replaced with an oil palm plantation.

Opposite: Lenny now safe in the arms of her COP rescuer.

Right: Lenny determined not to be left behind.

Buluc, an eighteen-month old male orangutan was found like this on an oil palm plantation camp in East Kalimantan.

Opposite: Aged about five or six *Memo* was rescued in Sebulu, East Kalimantan. A blood test later confirmed *Memo* is infected with Hepatitis B.

Safe now in the arms of his Ape Crusader rescuer. *Buluc* had machete wounds on his back which he would have received when in the arms of his mother as she was attacked and killed.

The owner of the orangutan receives a friendly reprimand from the local forestry police. Although illegal to possess or kill an orangutan, in the past 25 years about 75,000 have been killed without a single prosecution.

Buluc being safely carried ashore on his way to the rescue centre. Rescues often involve river crossings and long road trips.

Her owner had kept *Andrean* in this wooden cage for one month before she was rescued by COP's Ape Crusaders.

A hand. All that could be seen of *Andrean*.

Right: The caring hand of an Ape Crusader meets the human-like hand of the orangutan imprisoned in this makeshift cage.

Opposite: After one month in her 'coffin' *Andrean* was freed by COP.

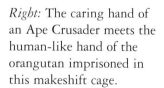

Coal mining is expanding rapidly throughout much of Kalimantan. Mining employees are often found in possession of baby orangutans. Australian mining companies are dominant in Eastern Kalimantan.

The rainforest about to be carried away and almost certainly ending up either as paper or furniture in shops not far from where you live.

Opposite: The price rainforests, orangutans and numerous other species pay for palm oil. How does this make you feel?

US$183 million: The value of the Norwegian State's investment in the five giant palm oil groups operating in Central Kalimantan without the necessary licenses.
Greenomics 2 March 2011

Right: If you look hard you can see young oil palm trees growing all over this land where rainforests once stood.

Work in progress – virtually every day of the year in Indonesia.

"To save the orangutan we have to save the forest,"
President Susilo Bambang Yudhoyono
December 2010, Bali Climate Change Conference

The Ape Crusader Rapid Reaction Team on their way to another rescue in Eastern Kalimantan in the four-wheel drive vehicle provided by Orangutan Appeal UK.

This new road is now the only thing to stand between the oil palm plantation to the right and what is left of this rainforest. Driven by hunger, orangutans often venture into oil palm plantations where they eat the tender young palms while risking death from oil palm workers if caught in the act.

Untung has good reason to look sad. He was clinging to his mother's warm chest when she was slashed to death with a machete. We know *Untung* was holding onto his mother when she was killed because during the onslaught he had two fingers of one hand chopped off.

Opposite: Untung enjoying milk for the first time since his mother was killed.

Despite being chained and clearly in danger of imminent death, the nearby Borneo Orangutan Survival Foundation giant rescue centre at Samboja Lestari refused to help this orangutan. It died one month later.

In October 2010 the Borneo Orangutan Survival Foundation (BOSF) did all they could to avoid helping three young orangutans rescued by COP and local forestry police.

At the time BOSF management and staff were enjoying their four-day conference at a nearby luxury hotel. Only after a highly critical public outcry did BOSF eventually relent and go to collect the orangutans – after their conference.

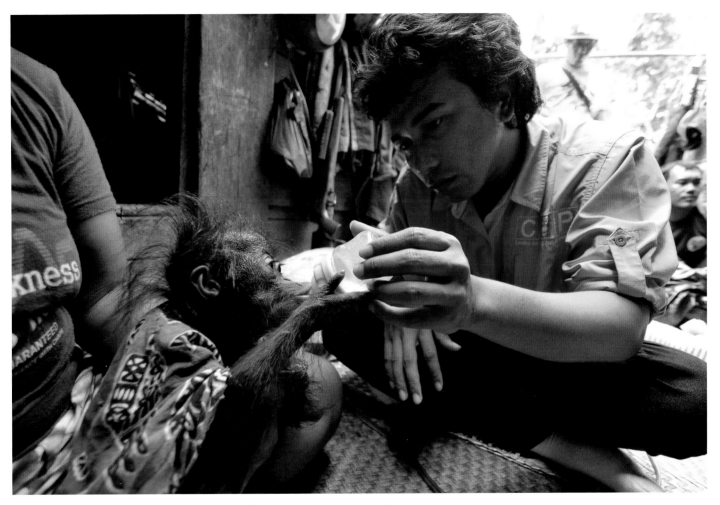

Cepot was eager to drink his first drop of milk since being removed from his mother's chest.

Opposite: Bewildered but about to be rescued, baby *Cepot* is one of thousands of orangutans orphaned or killed each year – and it has been this way for at least forty years.

It has been a long day but with *Alex* and *Kliwon* rescued and safely onboard the COP team are ready to leave Muara Wahau and head for the office of the forestry police in Samarinda, East Kalimantan.

The Kutai National Park, home to some 2000 orangutans in North East Kalimantan is supposed to be fully protected but homes and commercial development are rapidly encroaching upon the park.

It's impossible to even begin to imagine how many animals and birds lost their homes and lives when this forest was razed to the ground by a palm oil company.

More than 1,200 mining firms and 500 oil palm plantation companies operating illegally in Central, East and West Kalimantan provinces, on the Indonesian side of Borneo, are now being investigated by the Forestry Ministry.

"President Yudhoyono's eloquent words represent an important recognition by the Indonesian Government that preserving orangutan habitat is an environmental imperative, not only to protect this magnificent species from extinction but to help reduce carbon emissions resulting from the destruction of Indonesia's forests."

US Senator Patrick Leahy, Bali Climate Change Conference, December 2010

Hardi Baktiantoro comforts *Buluc*, a six month old male orangutan rescued from an oil palm plantation camp, East Kalimantan.

The smaller the size of the orangutan, the more desirable and expensive they are. Prices range from Rp500,000 to Rp2.5 million (approximately US$56-$278) each in Indonesia.

Center for Orangutan Protection (COP)

Thought to be about four years old *Keliu*
was a very frightened orangutan before she
was discovered like this and rescued by
Ape Crusaders in East Kalimantan.

Palm oil plantation workers are often found with baby orangutans, having already killed their mothers, which is why COP try to develop a good dialogue with plantation employees as well as to educate them about the protected status of orangutans.

The poster has a contact telephone number for people to call if they want an orangutan rescued.

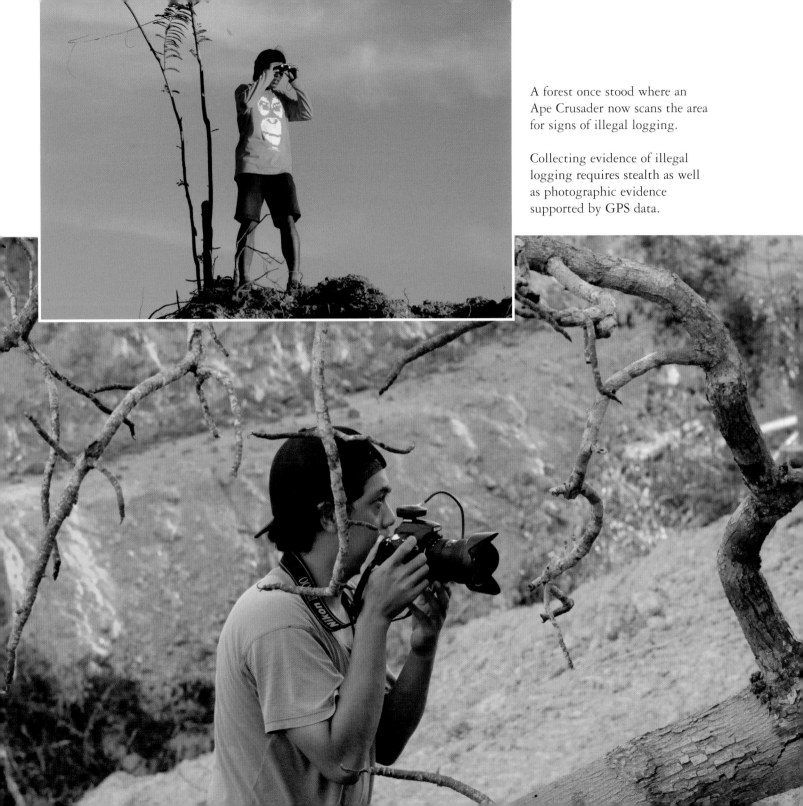

A forest once stood where an Ape Crusader now scans the area for signs of illegal logging.

Collecting evidence of illegal logging requires stealth as well as photographic evidence supported by GPS data.

The Ape Crusader team crossing a river in East Kalimantan on their way to rescue more orangutans.

A team of Ape Crusaders leaving a ferry and about to join a road still being built. The palm nuts to the left of the photo most probably fell from an overloaded truck while it was being loaded onto the ferry.

Local people are often employed to log their own ancestral forests. The offer of a job, however badly paid, to these people is better than no job at all. Only when the forest is gone do they appreciate what it provided for them by way of free food and clean water. Now they have to buy motorcycles to travel to shops a long way away to buy food, fuel and other every day needs the forests once provided for free and indefinitely.

Opposite: Whenever a call for help is received the Centre for Orangutan Protection (COP) can be relied upon to respond and help orangutans either wild or captive.

SUMATRA

Jambi, Sumatra. A hot-spot for deforestation.

Eyes on the Forest estimate that APP, which is owned by the multinational Sinar Mas conglomerate, and APRIL, which is owned by the Singapore-based Royal Golden Eagle Group, have together cleared roughly 2 million hectares of natural forests in Riau (Sumatra), accounting for nearly half the province's recent forest loss. Riau lost 4.4 million hectares of its 6.9 million hectares (63 percent) of forest cover between 1985 and 2009.

Jambi, Sumatra, where logging both legal and illegal continues at a breathtaking pace. Orangutans, tigers and elephants are all being driven from their forest homes and many are killed when they are forced to look for food close to human settlements.

JAVA

Bringing the desperate plight of orangutans to the capital city of Jakarta.

Opposite: COP consists of a small team of committed, passionate conservationists who rarely exceed 12 in number, including volunteers.

Placing great importance on education COP regularly attend schools including multi-national ones in the heart of Jakarta. Young children are always keen to learn about the orangutans and meet the people who devote their lives to saving them.

COP staff and volunteers receiving instruction on photography. COP have amassed approximately 10,000 photos documenting deforestation, oil palm plantations, illegally held orangutans and those held in zoos.

The Nature Resources Conservation Agency from the Ministry of Forestry and the Centre for Orangutan Protection (COP) joined forces on 3 March 2011 to confiscate a four year old female orangutan named *Rani* from a doctor who kept her as a pet at a maternity clinic in Cilacap, Central Java.

ZOOS

Pontianak Zoo,
West Kalimantan.

COP's vet at the time trying to comfort one of the orangutans kept in solitary confinement. This zoo was closed down shortly after complaints from both Nature Alert and COP about the conditions all the animals were held in.

The orangutan had been kept like this for a long time, unable to stand or climb, with only a bare wire floor to live and sleep on and no protection from either rain or sun.

Sinkawang Zoo in North West Kalimantan.

We discovered orangutans held in what can only be called barbaric cages at this zoo. Even if the zoo owner could have been persuaded to give them to a rescue centre, the nearest ones were already full and an extreme distance away. In the meantime the orangutans are either dying or going crazy held as they are in these all-wire cages day and night.

Most zoos throughout Indonesia keep their animals in barbaric conditions. Batu Raden Zoo in Java was no exception and has since been closed down.

Dreadful cages and a lack of food for the orangutans – boiled rice is often fed as it is cheap and plentiful. Water is rarely provided. Shelter from the searing daytime temperatures and monsoon-like rain is either inadequate or non-existent.

Opposite: Batu Raden Zoo. The expression on this orangutan's face says all there is to say about the lack of respect and humanity shown to this species in Indonesia. Look also at the skin condition of this individual and the decrepit state of its cage. A species which should be held as an icon of the environment in Indonesia, is instead reduced to this sorry state.

Above: Maharini Zoo, Java. Orangutans are often used as photo props. In exchange for payment these tourists have their photo taken with a very bored looking orangutan and live music played loudly in the background.

Left: Two orangutans share a tiny cage with a gibbon at the Romincy Water Park, Java.

Mankang Zoo, Java. Orangutans as well as other species have little to do all day but look out through the bars of their cages. They have nothing to climb on, nothing to play with and very little to live for. A common sight throughout Indonesian zoos.

To Indonesia's great shame, orangutans in the Ragunan (Jakarta) National Zoo have been held in cages like this for nearly twenty years, frequently kept short of food, water and often in solitary confinement.

Pekanbaru Zoo, Sumatra. *Gored*, a ten year old male orangutan clinging to life in his all-wire cage. He spends every day in a cage measuring approximately 2.5 square metres with no weather protection and nothing to sit on but a wet concrete floor.

Tina, a two year old orangutan claimed to have been born at the zoo. In her cage measuring approximately 2 x 1.5 x 1.5 meters she is constantly teased and tormented by visitors.

Tina smiling at her own reflection in the lens of a camera.

Lisa is said to be ten years old. Most of her life has been spent in this small cage at the Pekanbaru Zoo, Riau, Sumatra.

Before visiting any zoo Hardi always stops to buy fresh fruit and clean water for the orangutans.

Sanggau Zoo, North West Kalimantan. Despite numerous fresh fruit stalls nearby, these two orangutans are fed boiled rice and the occasional banana but no water. Look at the cage floor – this is where they live all day every day.

The Jakarta National Zoo is responsible for over twenty orangutans living in horrific conditions. For the past ten years many people have tried to help these orangutans, only to be thwarted by obstruction from zoo management and a disinterested government.

COP asking the Thai authorities to repatriate 12 orangutans stolen from Indonesia in 2010 and later discovered in Thailand. Inexplicably, the Indonesian government says it does not want the orangutans returned.

Safari World, Bangkok, Thailand, caught with 115 orangutans in 2003, was believed then to be the largest trader in illegally caught wild orangutans. For every orangutan which survives capture and shipping, it is thought another four to eight will have died. Safari World were never prosecuted but after a long campaign organized by Nature Alert, 48 orangutans were eventually returned to Indonesia in 2006.

The orangutans in these photos were most probably born in the forests of Indonesia and illegally shipped to Thailand via Malaysia.

Koh Kong Safari World, Cambodia. Some of their wild-caught orangutans illegally obtained between late 2004 and July 2006 from Safari World Bangkok, Thailand. Both countries are members of the Convention on International Trade in Endangered Species (CITES), but predictably CITES took no action against either country.